IMAGES
of America

NEW ENGLAND
SKIING
1870–1940

Tuckerman Ravine from Sherburne trail, Mt. Washington, New Hampshire, *c.* 1937.

IMAGES
of America

NEW ENGLAND
SKIING
1870–1940

E. John B. Allen

To Nancy,
Good skiing.
John Allen

ARCADIA

First published 1997
Copyright © E. John B. Allen, 1997

ISBN 0-7524-0494-6

Published by Arcadia Publishing,
an imprint of the Chalford Publishing Corporation,
One Washington Center, Dover, New Hampshire 03820.
Printed in Great Britain

Library of Congress Cataloging-in-Publication Data applied for

*Dedicated to all who have worked to preserve and display our
ski heritage in the New England Ski Museum.*

Contents

Acknowledgments

The collections of the New England Ski Museum in Franconia, New Hampshire, have provided one major source for this book. I should like to thank especially Linda Gray, executive director from 1989 to 1997, for her administrational help. I have also received courteous help from Karen S. Campbell, Bailey-Howe Library, University of Vermont; Susan Chandler, Brunswick, Maine; Rick Conard, B & M Railroad Historical Society, Lowell, Massachusetts; Philip N. Cronenwett, Dartmouth College, Hanover, New Hampshire; Sherman Howe, Friends of Woodstock Winters, Woodstock, Vermont; Edwin Lang, Stowe Historical Society, Stowe, Vermont; Karen McNulty, Hartland Historical Society, Hartland, Connecticut; Richard W. Moulton, Keystone Films, Huntington, Vermont; and Nicholas Noyes, Maine Historical Society, Portland. All have helped with images, and this selection would not have been possible without their interest and permission. I thank them all. Others who have also added to this book are Richard M. Chisholm, Rumney, New Hampshire; Glenn A. Parkinson, Gorham, Maine; and Wallace Stuart and R. Stuart Wallace, Plymouth, New Hampshire.

Introduction

In 1910, the *Boston Sunday Herald* interviewed Norwegian immigrant Dr. Andreas Christian, who rejoiced at the hundreds of skiers swarming over the suburban Newtons and Brooklines, Middlesex Falls, and Blue Hills. Skis were stacked on shop counters in Boston stores for people to enjoy the New Hampshire fields and dales 50 miles to the north, and the Berkshires were not to be belittled. The article was accompanied by eight large instructional photographs, and there were asides on the sport's appeal for children, its inexpensiveness, and its benefits to the physical and mental health of men. For women, Dr. Christian assured his readers, skiing was also "a great antidote for corsets."

It is difficult to believe Dr. Christian's assessment entirely, especially the number of participants and the availability of equipment, but it is no mistake that it was a Norwegian who was interviewed about skiing. It was, indeed, Scandinavians who had brought their 5,000-year-old ski culture with them to this country. The majority had settled in today's Midwest, but those who are pictorially documented here came to New England. The community of New Sweden in northern Maine was brought over from old Sweden in 1870 by Widgery Thomas, U.S. consul and later ambassador to Sweden. Norwegians came to work in the woods of Berlin, New Hampshire, for the Brown paper company, and Finns came to Maine and Newport, Vermont. Skiing spread throughout New England around the turn of the century thanks to the immigrant Scandinavians. Their sort of skiing was essentially utilitarian; for loggers, mailmen, and schoolchildren, it was a means of getting about at times of deep snows.

When some college men took up skiing, they turned it into a social sport. The Outing Club of Dartmouth College, founded in 1909, provided an impetus not only for the students and townspeople, but also for other colleges, towns, and villages which formed ski clubs from Maine to Connecticut and held competitions and carnivals in which the jump came to provide the greatest attraction. The images presented here try to demonstrate how an immigrant culture became an American sport.

In the 1930s, a second wave of skiing immigrants, this time from the European Alps, brought the thrill of speed to skiing. The Norse cross-country and jumping gave way to Alpine downhill and slalom. At the same time, the sport became mechanized. Snow trains brought a new, city clientele to the snowy hills, where tows of varying efficiency pulled the skiers to the top, and down they plunged on trails named to inspire derring-do: "Nose Dive," "Undertaker's Delight," and "Devil's Dip." These new-to-skiing folk needed to be taught how to manage a "schuss" and take a bump. Many "bended ze kneez" and happily paid their European instructors $2 for a lesson in the Arlberg technique, a low crouch and a lift and swing into the turn. Skiing in New England "took off" during the Depression. Once tows became established—we are talking here mostly about rope tows, as T-bars and chairlifts were rare prior to the Second World War—parking lots, restaurants, and inns all catered to the new and burgeoning winter business. Much of the labor of cutting trails was supplied by the Civilian Conservation Corps.

There seemed no end to the possibilities of enjoyment that skiing could bring. The selection of drawings, photographs, postcards, and posters covers the various facets of the 1930s. This is the period when the ski artists first came on the American scene, and Dwight Shepler's work is represented here. It is also the time when the journalists and photographers became important in spreading the joys of skiing. Look for the work of Christine Reid, Charles Trask, and Winston Pote. Maybe the most interesting photograph, historically, is that of Norman Libby, taken on Mt. Washington in 1907 and published here for the first time. Other rare photographs are the series on the construction of the Cannon Mountain tramway and the picture of Lowell Thomas leading a group of skiers into the Tuckerman Bowl.

The final chapter covers Mt. Washington, which first felt the skier's track in 1899. It was not until 1911 and 1912 that men entered the Bowl on skis, and did so regularly only from 1926 on. Mt. Washington, in winter, has remained untouched by mechanization to this day (the cog railway runs only in summer). In the 1930s, it was a spring rite of passage to climb up into the Bowl and picnic and socialize on Lunch Rocks in the sun.

The book ends with a poster which reflects a perfect spring day in Tuckerman. The war put this idyll on hold. The pictures capture some of the early winter sporting spirit and show how skiing as a necessity and pastime became a mechanized and modern sport.

E. John B. Allen

One

An Immigrant Import:
The Skee

"Skiing is one of our foreign imports which is absolutely unobjectionable."

—Leslie's Weekly, 1893.

Dr. F. Lawton leads Fred H. Harris at speed on a "slide" near Brattleboro, Vermont, about 1905.

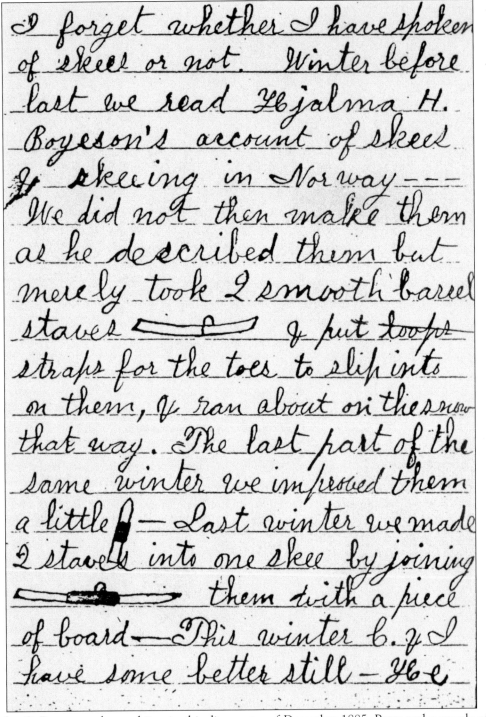

I forget whether I have spoken
of skees or not. Winter before
last we read Hjalma H.
Boyeson's account of skees
& skeeing in Norway ---
We did not then make them
as he described them but
merely took 2 smooth barrel
staves ⌣ & put loops
straps for the toes to slip into
on them, & ran about on the snow
that way. The last part of the
same winter we improved them
a little — Last winter we made
2 staves into one skee by joining
⎯ them with a piece
of board — This winter C. & I
have some better still — Se

John C. Perry remarks on skiing in this diary entry of December 1885. Perry and a couple of New Ipswich, New Hampshire friends made their own skis, bending the tips in his mother's washer. He went off to school and to the dentist on skis, and had "a genuine good time" with his friends.

This drawing of a New Hampshire school race in 1886 is quite correct in portraying the lone student on skis. Snowshoes were far more usual in New England until the 1920s.

There were no instructional manuals at the turn of the century. Instruction was by experience, and "two-on-a pole" proved a good way to learn how to ski.

These 1899 skis from Hartland, Connecticut, were hand-crafted by Norwegian immigrant Ole Simonsen for Willis L. Hayes, owner of the village store.

The popular look of a skier was portrayed in 1908 by a girl sporting a Harvard sweater. The college men took to the sport in the years before World War I, and college women did so in the 1920s.

Tumbles a-plenty there were in the early days off the jump, but few broken bones resulted, because the bindings consisted of nothing but a leather strap over the toes. Fred Harris rejoiced in getting distances of 40 and 45 feet.

Skiing down toboggan slides was not unusual in the years before World War I. The slide at St. Johnsbury, Vermont, attracted skiers c. 1890.

Maine's rural population was declining. In response, Widgery Thomas, recognizing Swedes as ideal settlers for Maine, brought over twenty-two men, eleven women, and eighteen children, who arrived on July 23, 1870, to create New Sweden.

This schoolhouse and the church were the first public buildings in New Sweden. In winter, children skied 5 miles across the countryside, "slipping over the snow on skidor, Swedish snowshoes," and left the skis lining the side of the building, "a strange sight in a Yankee school house."

At the Eagle Mountain House, in Jackson, New Hampshire, this threesome are trying out the meadows in 1887. A very few hostelries were open for winter business before 1900. They catered to the well-to-do from Boston. An Appalachian Mountain Club group on a snowshoe excursion might occasionally include a "skeeist," as at Fryeburg, Maine, in 1895.

In 1920, skiing was not quite as serious as Anna Hobbs makes it out to be. She is wearing her normal winter clothes, although the long skirt would soon disappear for winter activities. The long and hefty pole might be used for balance or even for braking speed, hobby-horse style.

Algernon G. Chandler owned the Bates College bookstore in Lewiston, Maine. He and Norman Libby of Bridgton made a 100-mile ski trip to Fryeburg and then up Mt. Washington in 1907. The large up-turn of the ski tip was designed to cope with the deep, unpacked snows of those years.

16

Theo. Johnsen of Portland, Maine, manufactured boats for summer enjoyment and skis for winter fun. He produced a fifty-four page ski catalog, of which thirty-four pages were devoted to instruction. "Skees" for youths, at 5 and 6 feet, for ladies at 7 feet, and men at 8 feet, were available, along with a variety of poles, including a locking pair. A skier's investment could range from $15 to $45—prices too high for the success of the firm, and Johnsen folded the business in 1907.

An illustration from the Johnsen catalog shows that the attractions of "downy, fluffy, powdery, sandy, dusty, flowery, crystalline, brittle, gelatinous, salt-like, slithery, and watery" snow were just as available to women as to men.

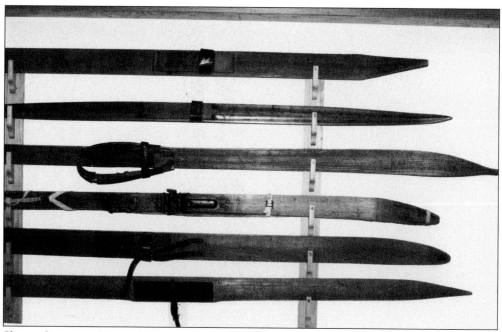

Shown here are skis used in New England from the late nineteenth century to 1920, on permanent display in the New England Ski Museum. Beginning at the top, the skis are as follows: 1] Typical utilitarian ski, c. 1900; 2] Ski made by Finnish immigrants; 3] Norwegian-type ski with a binding made from cane encased in leather; 4] Lilienfeld ski brought by an immigrant from Austria; 5 and 6] Examples of everyday skis used before 1920.

18

Forest Warden Frederick Jorgensen, originally from Sweden, worked in the Wilson Mills district of Maine in 1902. "The up-river gentry," as Jorgensen characterized poachers on their snowshoes, were in trouble with a warden able to cover 50 miles in good going. Jorgensen's skis became an "everlasting trade mark . . . When people saw my tracks it was as if a loud speaker had announced over the countryside, The Warden is Coming!"

Algernon Chandler enjoyed skiing with his friends on Pleasant Mountain, Maine. The wealthier sectors of society began to take to skiing around the turn of the century, purely for sport.

Little by little, enough winter enthusiasts created a clientele for the inns to remain open for the snow and ice season.

The Hanover Inn used its connections with Dartmouth outdoorsmen reveling in the snow to advertise its readiness to receive winter guests.

Finns also emigrated to communities from Massachusetts to Maine. Theo. Johnsen actually prepared advertisements for his skis in Finnish. This homemade pair of long, thin skis was made by pulp cutters in either Dover or Wilmington, Vermont, around the turn of the century.

An immigrant in New Britain, Connecticut, in 1910 inspired his high school students to make skis and then try them out. This group on the Manchester, Connecticut golf course is having a high old time, together with a lot of spectators watching the frolics.

Two
Clubs and Carnivals: Organizing Skiing

"The business of the ski club shall be in the Norwegian language only. Any Scandinavian of good reputation over 15 will be accepted by majority vote. If a member is drunk he cannot participate."

—Translated from the Constitution of the Fridtjof Nansen Ski Club,
Berlin, New Hampshire, 1907.

This is the first formal photograph of the Dartmouth Outing Club which Fred Harris (center) proposed on November 30, 1909, to stimulate an interest in winter sports. Dartmouth "might well become the originator of a branch of college organized sport hitherto undeveloped by American colleges."

OUTING CLUB
CROSS COUNTRY TRIP
OVER BALD HILL
TO W. R. Return ON 4.50 train
BRING CAMERAS.

In about 1910, the Dartmouth Outing Club announced a cross-country ski trip leaving the college for Bald Hill and ending at White River Junction, Vermont. One of the attractions—besides the camaraderie—was cross-country's work ethic; the more miles you accomplished, the more moral you became! Harris skied 98 miles in the winter of 1910–11.

Of these five DOC members, two have no poles, and the rest use two each, c. 1915. In the early days, to ski without poles was the mark of an expert. Most skied with a single staff. One Dartmouth student tried out two poles at dusk so no one would see him; he did not wish to be thought effeminate.

24

Nansen Club Juniors pose at an away meet against Eaglebrook School, Deerfield, Massachusetts: Elmer Hermanson, Howard Nelson, Lawrence Barbin, Henry Barbin, Roland Rasmusson, Albert Barbin, Irving Mann, and Robert Mortenson. Note that Scandinavian names were still prominent in the late 1920s.

World-renowned for his crossing of Greenland on skis in 1888, and later for his Arctic explorations (besides his work for displaced persons after World War I), Dr. Fridtjof Nansen came to Berlin, New Hampshire, in 1929. He was escorted from the station by the Nansen Club Juniors. The five men at the top are Major McGee, Nansen, Mr. Christianson, Mr. Graf, Mr. Gordon Brown of the Brown Company, and Mr. Alf Halvorsen, the main promoter of the Nansen Club for many years.

Proudly wearing his Nansen Ski Club sweater, this Berlin, New Hampshire lad is getting set for his turn on the jump. From small neighborhood jumps, boys migrated to the jump on Payne's meadow before the towering structure on the Milan road was ready for the 1938 season.

Part of the carnival fun on skis was the obstacle race. Here, Berlin schoolchildren crawl through barrels—quite tricky on skis longer than 5 feet.

A skiing party took to the snows around the Poland Spring Hotel, Maine. The owner had wintered in Europe in 1913, "taking notes with a view to developing winter sports on a large scale."

Dover, New Hampshire lads were all dressed up for meet day, c. 1921. Clubs proliferated all over New England in the 1920s and 1930s. They held local competitions, built jumps, and sponsored carnivals.

The interscholastic prep school meet was held in Brattleboro, Vermont, c. 1930. Roger Langley, seated third from right, then a master at Eaglebrook, would later serve for many years as secretary of the National Ski Association. In the 1920s, Eaglebrook, Cushing, St. Johnsbury, Hebron, New Hampton, and Norwood were regular competitors. They were joined in the 1930s by Mt. Hermon, Vermont Academy (whose carnival pre-dated Dartmouth's), Hotchkiss, Clark, Deerfield, St. Mark's, Middlesex, Leland-Grey, Choate, and St. Paul's.

Fred Harris, Dartmouth Class of 1911, pauses with physics professor Proctor. Proctor, a keen supporter of the DOC and the Intercollegiate Ski Association (founded in 1921), was an influential jumping judge and the father of 1928 Olympian Charley Proctor. In 1914, Prof. Proctor was one of the first skiers up Dartmouth's own Mt. Moosilauke.

With his "loop-the-loop" during intermission at the intensely serious jumping competition at the Dartmouth Winter Carnival, Gustav Poulson from Berlin, New Hampshire, was a regular performer for a number of years starting in 1917.

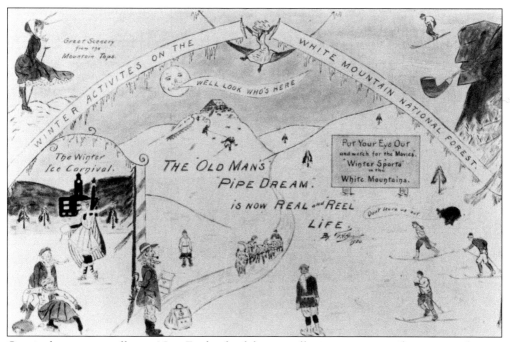

Carnivals sprang up all over New England celebrating all winter sports—tobogganing, skating, curling, dog sledding, snowshoeing, and skiing. This drawing comes from Gorham, New Hampshire, c. 1930.

The Hanover, New Hampshire common formed a perfect venue, whether for an elegant trot or a fast-paced race. Ski-joring came from a European military background: the Scandinavian and Swiss armies trained soldiers as dispatch couriers. Being pulled along behind horses became popular among the wealthy tourists at St. Moritz in Switzerland. In this country, the sport never achieved general popularity, but it did provide spills and thrills a-plenty on carnival day.

"Stowe knows how to DO things." The first carnival in 1921 featured an ice palace constructed behind the high school. Under lights, Eskimo Pies, doughnuts, coffee, and cider were served.

Stowe's main street provided the course for "snake racing"—toboggans pulled behind a tractor. Most impressive of all was Horace Melendy of Jeffersonville, Vermont, being towed behind a car at 35 mph. (Locals will realize this photograph is printed backwards.)

The king and queen (Major E.E. Philbrook and Miss Winona Drew) of the 1924 Portland, Maine Winter Carnival, along with their pages, led a parade to an outdoor party at Deering Oaks park to open the carnival festivities.

The USEASA, more often called "Eastern," was founded in 1922 with seven member clubs. There were 38 in 1930, 112 by 1935, and 181 in 1940. The logo of the jumper indicates the powerful presence of the Norwegian tradition into the 1920s.

Three
Knights of the Air:
Jumping

"At best, all other forms of ski-sport must remain a dull and uninteresting rival for the gagging thrill of the ski-jumpers' soaring flight . . . to the flat at the very feet of the spectators."

—Literary Digest, 1934.

A competitor in the 1938 meet at Brattleboro, Vermont, displays the style of the day.

In early ski jumping meets, the "squat jump," shown here by Fred Harris, c. 1910, was one accepted style, but it soon gave way to the more graceful upright bend into the wind.

In this photograph from 1911, Harris is jumping upright off a homemade jump at Dartmouth, but he is not yet leaning forward in order to ride the air efficiently.

Jumping turned skiing into a national spectator sport. Huge crowds came to watch the stars: 3,000 in Brattleboro, Vermont, in 1924; 6,000 in Salisbury, Connecticut, in 1933; and 25,000 in Berlin, New Hampshire, in 1938.

This scene on the Manchester, Connecticut golf course is typical of the 1920s small town club action on homemade jumps.

From this wooden structure, built for the Portland, Maine Winter Carnival of 1924, the winner jumped 91 feet, tantalizingly near the magic 100! Competitors from Berlin, New Hampshire, and Rumford, Maine, were particularly in evidence, besides the local heroes, the Olsens. The spirit of "citius, altius, fortius"—swifter, higher, stronger—from the Olympic Games permeated all sports in the 1920s.

Colebrook Carnival · 1925

To many people in the 1920s, skiing was jumping. Every town's carnival included a jump, which was the climax of the two-day program.

National jumping competitions all took place in the Norwegian-dominated Midwestern ski communities until Brattleboro, Vermont, hosted the National Championship for the first time in the eastern United States in 1924. This dual jump provided an entr'acte between the serious competitive jumps.

In 1922, Bing Anderson, Berlin's most well-known jumper, gained firsts at Berlin and Conway, New Hampshire; Stowe and Brattleboro, Vermont; Saranac Lake and Lake Placid, New York; a second at Portland, Maine; and a third at Ottawa, Canada. In 1923, Anderson won firsts at Brattleboro, and in New Hampshire at Bristol and Berlin, and a second at Revelstoke in British Columbia, Canada.

The best-known jump in southern New England was in Salisbury, Connecticut, home to the three Satre brothers from Norway.

Salisbury's jump was considered sophisticated enough to be chosen for the 30th National Ski Jumping Championship in 1933.

The best jumps were built to conform with the topography. In Maine, Rumford's hugged the hill nicely, and at the same time the trees protected the jumper from side winds.

Not a particularly polished launch from the platform! The take-off was vital to ensure a good style in the air, so one would receive high marks from the judges. These were added to the distance points.

Bing Anderson is about to lean into the wind. This jump netted him an Eastern record of 152 feet in 1924.

Double jumps like this one at Berlin, New Hampshire, were crowd pleasers. Sometimes jumpers would go off hand in hand. Triple jumps were not unknown. It was all part of the ski show, and attracted non-skiers to venture out and watch the intrepid Vikings of the Sky.

New Hampshire's other jump was built at the Belknap Recreation Area in Gilford during the Depression by Civilian Conservation Corps labor.

The Belknap Recreation Area sponsored summer ski jumping in 1938, which pulled in the crowds. In the 1930s, skiing on sand dunes, on pine needles, and on straw was tried—on the whole without much success.

The great 60-meter jump at Berlin (now in decay) was dedicated on March 7, 1938. On that day Clarence "Spike" Oleson jumped 180 feet in front of 25,000 spectators. The longest distance was achieved by Ansten Samuelsten with 262 feet. Later, the jump was altered slightly, and Christian Berrgrav sailed to a new record of 271 feet in 1976.

OPENING

World's
Largest
Ski Tower

OLYMPIC TRYOUTS

SATURDAY and SUNDAY
March Fifth and Sixth

1938

Berlin's jump was considered one of the best in North America. It received national recognition with the tryouts for the Olympic Games scheduled for 1940. These competitions would be canceled because of the outbreak of war.

A Nazi flag flies at Brattleboro, Vermont, in recognition of a visiting German team in 1938. The flag caused disruptions and there were several attempts to pull it down.

Torger Tokle arrived from Norway in January 1939. He electrified easterners with his jumping: forty-two firsts out of forty-eight competitions, and he set ten hill records. Here he is receiving the Silver Wings trophy from Fred Harris at Brattleboro, before joining the US Army in October 1942. He was killed by artillery fire in Italy.

Four

Tools of the Season: Marketing the Magic

"If the back end of the ski becomes broken cut it off straight. If a crack appears make a small hole at each end of the crack and plug it with wax. This will prevent it from spreading."

—Anton Diettrich, Dartmouth's first coach, 1924.

The Poland Spring brochure for 1920 billed winter as "the season for ringing sport and jollity in Maine . . . of invigorating cold . . . and throngs of frolicing guests . . . in the land of health and vigor which is Maine."

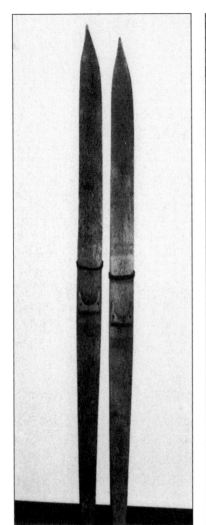

There was an enormous variety of skis in the early days. Very rough and ready boards (like the ones on the left in Damariscotta, Maine, in 1895) would be used on a farm, whereas skis of unequal length (like the ones on the right, outside the New Sweden Historical Museum) were made by immigrants, in a style similar to what they had known at home. The shorter ski, often covered with seal skin, was for pushing, the longer one for gliding. The last maker of unequal skis in New Sweden was Henry Anderson, who had begun his craft in 1926. In Scandinavia, the skis had a greater difference in length; more typical over here was a one or two foot difference.

Theo. Johnsen of Portland (see p. 17) was out of business by 1907. Paris Manufacturing, in Paris, Maine, began to compete with the bigger Midwestern companies of Strand and Northland in the 1920s. The Paris skis were flat-topped and cheap, built of pine and ash mostly. Hickory was more expensive. Henry Morton remembered hunting out little backwoods mills in the southern US for satisfactory hickory billets in the 1930s. A leather thong pulled through a mortise sufficed for a binding. A rubber platform underfoot prevented the snow from building up, and sometimes a wooden block helped to keep the foot in place.

These homemade "riggings," as bindings were often called at the turn of the century, were made in 1899 in Connecticut. They were very simple: the boot was pushed under the toe strap and the thong buckled behind the heel, keeping the foot in place—sort of—but allowing the heel to move freely.

This binding exhibit is on view in the New England Ski Museum. The bindings are, from left to right, as follows: 1] Very simple *c.* 1900 toe strap and heel thong construction, after a Norwegian model; 2] Iron heel holder made by a farrier in Brattleboro, Vermont; 3+4] Metal flanges on either side with an adjustable leather strap over the top hold the forefoot firmly in place (a wooden block is located under the heel); 5] Further improvement in heel fastening—the heel strap is hinged to the toe plate; 6] The Amstutz spring, strapped around the ankle and attached to the ski approximately 10 inches behind the heel. The Amstutz spring was popular with the expert skier of the 1930s. It held the heel down for control during turns while it allowed for some give for a strong forward lean, both so vital in the Arlberg technique.

Shown here is a joke: 42-foot skis at Plymouth, New Hampshire, for advertising the town as the "Snow Bowl of the East" in the 1930s.

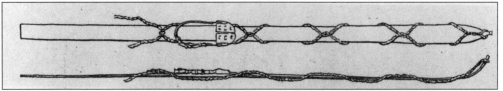

Skins strapped to the bottom of the skis—seal skin was preferred—prevented the skis from slipping backwards on a climb, the only uphill mode before the rope tow era. A cheaper alternative was to tie a rope in the manner pictured.

After the advent of rope tows (1934), a variety of rope tow grippers came on the market. This one, from Bousquet's in the Berkshires, is a very sophisticated belt. In Maine, a notched paddle-like board could be bought, and a kind of steel claw was available in New Hampshire.

Wax often won races, and waxing was considered an art in the 1920s and 1930s. Imported waxes from Norway were favored in the 1920s, and Sohm's became the wax of choice in the 1930s, with various colors for particular types of snow.

Shown here is the complete skier, c. 1930. Ski tips out of sight, adjustable bear-trap bindings, long bamboo poles with huge baskets, and isn't this skieuse wearing a fancy outfit! But then—she is on her honeymoon.

SKIING

CLOTHING
to prevent chills

EQUIPMENT
to provide thrills

Hickory ridge top Slalom, Touring and Down-
  hill skis $16
Ash, edge grain, ridge top $12
Hard rock maple, ridge top $9
Hickory, flat-top Touring $9.50
Ash, edge grain $7.50, $8
Maple, hard rock, 5ft. to 7½ ft. .... $4 to $6.50
Pine, 4ft. to 6½ ft. .... $1.25 to $3.25
Ski poles ...... $2.75 to $5 pr. Youth's ... $1.50 pr.
Waxes ...... 25c to 50c Bindings .... $3 to $7.50
Ski Boots .. $5.85 to $10. Ski Socks 75c to $1.75.
Wind-proof Parkas .... $5. up
Ski Breeches .... $5. to $10. Ski Caps .... $1.75.

Shoe Skates Hockey Tube 5⁴⁵

Other Hockey Shoe Skates .... $8.95 to $24.50
Figure Shoe Skates .... $8.95 to $27.35
Snow Shoes .... $3.85 to $12
Snow Shoe Sandals .... $1.50 and $1.75

SKATES SHARPENED—Regular Grind, 25c; Oil Finish, 50c.
SKIS RECONDITIONED

*For authentic Ski clothing and equip-
ment — come to Wright & Ditson*

Wright & Ditson
344 Washington St., Boston
Tel. LIBerty 2733

Wright and Ditson, well-known as purveyors of tennis gear, diversified their sporting offerings to include winter activities. This 1936 advertisement illustrates the range of skis available.

Wendelin Hilty came to Plymouth, New Hampshire, from Switzerland via instructing the Chilean army. Part of the marketing of skiing was the image presented by the resident expert, and being Swiss equaled authority in the skiing world of the 1930s.

52

Increasingly, hotels began to remain open over the winter. This brochure from 1924 listed over ninety hotels in various skiing venues: two in Maine, thirty in New Hampshire, twelve in Vermont, and eleven in Massachusetts.

The New England Ski Museum in Franconia, New Hampshire exhibits a range of skis, c. 1900–40, from its collection.

The Original New England Ski Feature

Originated, Edited and Read by Ski Enthusiasts

"OLD MAN·WINTER"

The live, authoritative weekly feature on which New England skiers have depended for six years. Read "Old Man Winter" for authentic up-to-the-minute information on weather and snow conditions, trails, tows, competitions, club meetings, and other Winter Sports events. Follow the news and advertising for latest dope on new equipment, transportation, and places to go. The active skier finds "Old Man Winter" an essential to his season's enjoyment.

75¢ for 15 consecutive issues, single copies 5¢ by mail

*Published Every Friday
November 26 through March 25
Only in the*

Boston Evening Transcript

Boston   Massachusett

The ski journalist is a product of alpine skiing. People had to be told where to go, how to ski, what to wear, what to buy, and even what to say: "Ski Heil" was the greeting. The phrase indicated the switch from the Nordic world of cross-country to the German schuss.

Two ski shops opened in Boston in the late 1920s: Asa Osborn's, and the one shown here, Oscar Hambro's. Skiers regarded them as clubs as much as shops, swapping information on equipment or deciding on snow train destinations. Christine Reid, photographer and journalist, can be recognized on the left, with ski instructor Ed Boeck on the right.

The New Hampshire booth at the 1938 Sportsman's Show in Boston portrayed the charms of the lumber country now combining with the new first-in-the-nation "Skyway to Ski Fun," the Cannon mountain tramway, at 60¢ a ride.

Competition among the New England states for skiers from the cities brought about state advertising. In Massachusetts, there is a Geländesprung for the expert, a social time awaits the well-dressed gal, and there are cross-country delights for all.

Equipment, fashion, hotels, inns, hostels, restaurants, and railroads, all were put on view at the annual ski shows, first in Boston in 1935, then also in Madison Square Garden in New York. Thousands of spectators watched demonstrations of skiing and ski jumping on crushed ice.

The ski shows—and some carnivals, as shown here in 1935—often ended with a leap through a hoop of fire. Miraculous to some, it appeared as "show-biz" to others.

Five
Fashion for Snow Frolics: Winter Togs

"Do not wear too vivid colors. The brilliant plumage of a parrot does not fit well in a snow landscape."

—Anton Diettrich, 1924.

This was quite the outfit for indoor pre-season training! Miles Bartlett of the Greylock ski club receives instruction from Joseph Aspinall at the Boston YMCA gymnasium in 1937.

The north country girls were ready for the Berlin carnival, *c.* 1920. These are the right clothes for winter shopping, snowshoeing, skating, skiing, and carnival watching. After the Great War, women could wear sporting pants, rather than the long skirts of the earlier days.

We are quite prepared to admire what ski experts were wearing around 1920 in Manchester, Connecticut. The long scarf was a symbol of winter. Of course, you could wrap yourself up in its warmth, but it was far better to have it streaming behind you as you raced down the slope.

A Dartmouth beau and his belle were photographed during the Winter Carnival of 1913. Winter carnivals rivaled spring proms in popularity.

Appalachian Mountain Club members enjoyed a healthy pace on an outing in the late 1920s, striding out and looking fine. For some, their riding jodhpurs appear to be doing duty as ski pants.

In 1929, a group from Boston disembarked at the head of the Wapack trail in Massachusetts, one of the first cared for and brush-cut for skiing by the AMC. The "Appies" played a major role in the development of New England skiing through projects such as trail work, sponsorship of dry-course training, hiring experts, and organizing snow trains.

Oscar H. Hambro Co.

Hickory Skis
  Norwegian
  Swiss
  Hambro's
  Domestic

Ski Bindings
  Ski-Craft
  Kandahar
  Other Imported
    and Domestic

Bildstein Springs

Ski Clothing
  Gabardines
  Woolens
  English Fabrics

Ski Boots
  Imported and Domestic

Ski Poles

Ski Wax

Sealskins

Plush Creepers

Ski Packs
  and Knapsacks

Faltboats
  European Type

SKI-CRAFT
MAKERS OF FINER SKI EQUIPMENT

17 CARVER STREET, BOSTON
(Off Park Square)

448 LEXINGTON AVENUE, NEW YORK CITY
(Near Grand Central Station)

FACTORY AT EAST RINDGE, N. H.

Oscar Hambro opened his shop in Boston in 1926. His was the first to survive the winter on selling ski equipment and clothing only. In the other seasons, Hambro manufactured and sold canoes and paddles. This is a 1937 advertisement.

This 1936 advertisement for the Murren suit had snob appeal: wealthy Americans journeyed to this Swiss resort to learn how to ski and how to enjoy social skiing à la British. At the same time, C. Crawford Hollidge was still appealing to the Norse heritage: "Skoal! say the Northmen." Or does he not know the difference?

"*Murren*"

25.00

"Skoal!" say the Northmen in toast to this suit that complies with vim and vigor to the rules of the game. Cravenetted worsted gabardine—which means it's light, windproof and waterproof. Impeccably tailored with plus fours that are perfection plus, with leather epaulettes and buttons—which means

These fellows going skiing on the Thunderbolt trail at Mt. Greylock, Massachusetts, have obviously been shopping at a classy ski emporium for their jackets, trousers, puttees, and downhill ski equipment.

In 1937, this impressive skier's excellent choice of clothes was matched by his accomplished slalom technique, as he flashed down between the small flags that marked the course.

Being or just looking European carried automatic credentials in the 1930s ski schools. Norman Dyhrenfurth taught with Roger Peabody in Franconia, New Hampshire, in 1938. He would later make a name for himself as cinematographer and mountaineer; he led the team which put the first Americans on Mt. Everest in 1963.

Peckett's, an expensive hostelry on Sugar Hill, New Hampshire, catered to expensive people dressed in expensive clothes, such as this lady posing in the sun and snow of the White Mountains.

Rudolf
Friedrich
at St. Anton
on the
Arlberg . . .

Rudolf Friedrich

OUR SKI INSTRUCTOR DIRECT FROM THE AUSTRIAN ALPS—WILL EXHIBIT AT THE

National Winter Sports

Exposition and Ski Tournament

In Boston Garden—November 29-December 6

When not going off the steep end of the great indoor slide during the Ski competitions at the Garden Snow Sports Show, Mr. Friedrich will be in our "White Horse Inn" Ski Shop there, to give you tips on everything from correct Christys to correct clothes to wear when making them. Enroll for Mr. Friedrich's classes for Ski Gymnastics ($1 each lesson) at our own indoor ski slide on the second floor, main store—or at our Ski Shop in Boston Garden.

Visit "White Horse Inn" in our Tyrolean Village, Second Floor—Main Store.

Visit Jordan's "White Horse Inn" Ski Shop at the Boston Garden Winter Sports Show.

Six shops for Snow Sports—wearables for tots, girls, boys, men, women and all the equipment for everyone!

This advertisement for the Boston Garden Ski Show of 1936 shows how the European ambiance attracted attention: Rudolf Friedrich is "direct from the Austrian Alps." He comes from St. Anton, home to Hannes Schneider, Skimeister to the world. He will teach you "Christys" after you have visited the inn in "our Tyrolean Village."

Two of the great personages of New England skiing appear like fashion models in this 1939 photograph. Sig Buchmayr, one-time resident impresario at Peckett's, wears the required European costume of the day. Hannes Schneider, the Alpine world's most renowned teacher, is wearing boots named for him. The boots were made by another immigrant, Peter Limmer.

WINTER
IN · NEW ENGLAND

Gone were the days of using ordinary winter wear and rough boots. The 1930s saw an explosion of ski fashion. For the wealthy, ski costume designers produced annual changes. Winter in New England was not merely for skiing, but for social skiing.

Six

Bend ze Kneez: Arlberg Instruction

"Let's not permit international bickering and national jealousies to thrive on anything so splendid as skiing. Let's ski for fun, and learn what we can from our cousins across the water, so long as they don't make the learning process a chore."

—Lowell Thomas, 1937.

Otto Schniebs from Germany taught the AMC to snowplow in the 1928–29 season. "His unusual skill as an instructor, made the more effective by his engaging personality, and the brilliance of his own example have brought scores of learners to . . . the supple crouch, with its elastic knee, and the easy rhythmical Christiania." (AMC Report, 1929.)

Peckett's, on Sugar Hill, New Hampshire, is considered the place where American ski schools got their start in 1929. Every morning, the instructors—they were called trainers to begin with—began with twenty to thirty minutes of calisthenics on skis, before launching into the Arlberg technique.

A long line of European instructors taught skiing all over New England. Here Florian Haemmerle, suitably eccentric, "bends ze kneez" for the Hanover Inn.

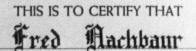

THIS IS TO CERTIFY THAT

Fred Nachbaur

HAS BEEN EXAMINED IN ACCORDANCE WITH THE

PROVISIONS FOR THE CERTIFICATION OF SKI TEACHERS

OF THE

UNITED STATES EASTERN AMATEUR SKI ASSOCIATION

AND HAS BEEN FOUND

QUALIFIED AND COMPETENT

TO GIVE INSTRUCTION IN SKIING

(CHAIRMAN, COMMITTEE ON THE CERTIFICATION OF SKI TEACHERS)

(EXAMINER)

APPROVED

(PRESIDENT, U. S. E. A. S. A.)

After four years of discussion, the United States Eastern Amateur Ski Association held its first examination for professional instructors on February 14, 1938, at Woodstock, Vermont. Seven men passed. By the 1939–40 season, three women had become certified.

Skiing Fun in New Hampshire—a High Speed Christi Turn

Fred Nachbaur, American-born but fluent in German, was once refused a ski instructor's job because he did not have enough of an accent! Nachbaur became a major influence on skiing in the Gilford, New Hampshire area.

"The Austrian Instructor" arrived in Stowe, Vermont, in 1936, and immediately advocated cutting down more trees for open slope skiing. Sepp Ruschp remained in Stowe until his death in 1990.

AUSTRIAN INSTRUCTOR

MT. MANSFIELD

Sepp Ruschp taught the Arlberg technique in his Arlberg outfit, including the Tyrolean hat. Vermont ski centers were slow off the mark to develop, partially because the state's attorney general had said in 1937 that paid admission for skiing was against the law on Sundays. A state of Vermont assessment for the 1937–38 season concluded that it was still questionable whether skiing was going to be a permanent factor in the state.

70

EASTERN SLOPE

SKI SCHOOL
BENNO RYBIZKA
DIRECTOR

AMERICAN BRANCH OF THE HANNES SCHNEIDER

SKI SCHOOL

P.O. JACKSON or NORTH CONWAY, N.H.

The Arlberg teaching and technique became entrenched in New England, with Benno Rybizka as guardian of the American branch. According to one of his instructors, he ran the ski school like a Prussian general. But the clients kept coming. Ski school was almost a requirement for the beginner.

Hannes Schneider (right), with Benno Rybizka at his side, arrived in North Conway in 1939. He had been under house arrest in Germany because he had supported a Jewish member of the Austrian Ski Association. Harvey Gibson's money—he was president of the Hanover Trust—and pressure from Arnold Lunn, co-founder with Schneider of the Arlberg-Kandahar race, finally extricated him from the Nazis. He made his home in North Conway until he died in 1955.

Hannes Schneider is seen leading his instructors down the open slope at Mt. Cranmore, New Hampshire.

On the back of this postcard was written, "I actually saw him doing this!!" Instructors were the stars of 1930s skiing, and it was essential that periodically they show off their skills.

Here, the Skimeister instructs the instructors, although a couple do not seem to be paying much attention! Mt. Cranmore's skimobile is in the background.

One necessity for all beginners was to learn how to herringbone up a hill. The skier on the left is sidestepping.

To raise the standard of club skiing, Otto Schniebs gave a course for club instructors (i.e., non-professionals) in 1938. This group is a who's who of New England skiing. Among them are: (far left) Park Carpenter, AMC and snow train organizer; (seventh from left) H.H. Whitney, owner of a ski lodge and center in Jackson, New Hampshire, and inventor of the "shovel handle lift"; (ninth from left) J.W. McCrillis, co-author, with Otto Schniebs (third from right) of one of the most popular instructional books.

Otto Schniebs, coach at Dartmouth from 1931 to 1936, seemed to electrify the Hanover community with the new Arlberg technique. One erring student once executed a perfect Norwegian telemark turn. "Don't ever let me see you make that turn again," admonished Otto, "dot is a lady's turn." His fractured English became part of the Schniebs lore. When asked what to do if conditions were awful, he replied, "Vell, either take the damned skis off and valk—or schtem—schtem like hell!"

In typical organized, even military line-up, a Cannon Mountain class watched Hans Thorner's demonstration of the pole plant.

Here, Sepp Ruschp leads his "Hot Four." From left to right are Kerr Sparks, Howard Moody, Lionel Hayes, and Otto Hollaus. Compare this photograph with the first pictures of "the Austrian Instructor" on p. 70. By 1940, Sepp had his ski school, its students, distinctive in their sweaters and caps, organized along modern, American lines, yet looking European.

Hans Thorner from Switzerland, among the seven who were first certified as instructors in the United States, parlayed his expertise into this advertisement for Camel cigarettes in the late 1930s.

The perfect instructor, impeccably dressed, Franz Koessler demonstrates a stem turn in 1938.

Seven
Have a Glorious Sun-day: Snow Trains

"It was truly a gathering of red blooded, clean, wholesome lovers of winter sports."

—Olive Anson on her first snow train outing, 1933.

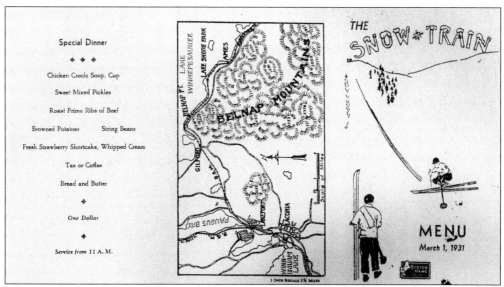

Special Dinner

♦ ♦ ♦

Chicken Creole Soup, Cup

Sweet Mixed Pickles

Roast Prime Ribs of Beef

Browned Potatoes   String Beans

Fresh Strawberry Shortcake, Whipped Cream

Tea or Coffee

Bread and Butter

♦

One Dollar

♦

Service from 11 A. M.

THE SNOW TRAIN
MENU
March 1, 1931

Snow trains became a regular part of the ski season starting in 1931, when 197 enthusiasts descended on Warner, New Hampshire on January 11. The B & M Railroad carried 8,371 people from Boston that first season. The "Special Dinner" was available to 980 passengers bound for Laconia in March.

In 1907 the B & M had tried to promote the "Winter Vacation Habit" by getting people snowshoeing, skiing, skating, and tobogganing. In the 1920s, as this employees' magazine cover shows, there was an appeal to the skier to watch "the breathtaking thrill of the ski jumping contests with the daring leap from dizzy heights."

At Grand Central Station, New York, weekend skiers boarded the overnight "Ski Meister" bound for New Hampshire and Vermont. The scene attracted curious spectators in crowds so large that the authorities had to rope off an area for them.

When the ski crowd arrived at an out-of-the-way village, the train remained in the station available for rest and recuperation, "a club house for naps between exhilarating and strenuous exercise." It was a place to eat lunch and leave your belongings. Après ski song fests often continued as the train tracked back to the city, especially in cars hired by a club.

The B & M snow train to the White Mountains in New Hampshire was such a success that the railroad tried it to Poland Spring, Maine, in 1932. The beginning of the ski package can be seen in this advertisement: $21.96 not only bought you the round trip from Boston but also two days of skiing at the Poland Spring Hotel.

Out they poured! The "experts" would try the local mountain, the intermediates found a nearby meadow to practice their glides, and the beginners had club instruction. That first season, on Washington's Birthday in 1931, 1,762 people took the train to Wilton, New Hampshire, and 2,058 went to Woodstock, New Hampshire, in 1933.

In 1936, the American Ski Annual provided exposure for advertisers such as the New Haven Railroad, which ran regular service to the Berkshires. The train also stopped at White River Junction, Vermont, for Hanover, New Hampshire, and at Waterbury, Vermont, from where a tram, the Toonerville Trolley, took skiers to Stowe.

Some snow trains had equipment and even clothes on board for rent or sale. The service car was also used to wax and repair skis. The cheaper skis, those with knots in them, broke easily. A prepared skier might carry an aluminum tip to make an on-the-hill mend, but then he or she would come in to the train for the professional repair work to be done.

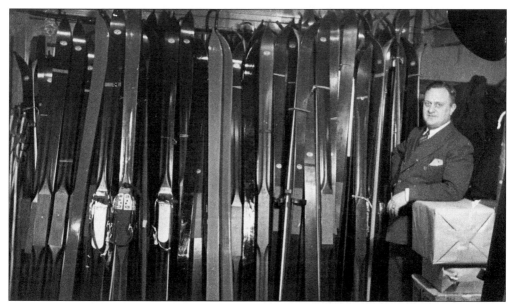

General Manager Sam Auerbach proudly displayed his selection of equipment. It was a worthwhile undertaking, since so many beginners rode the snow trains.

Sam Auerbach insures that a couple of "snow bunnies" will have a perfect day. The snow train sign may promise the cold of the northern hills, but on the B & M it was warm enough for these two to be in shirts and sweaters.

B & M's magazine cover for January-February 1933 depicted well-dressed skiers. It turned out to be a comparatively snowless year. The B & M carried 7,703 passengers that season compared to 14,974 in 1934, 17,943 in 1935, and 24,240 in 1936. Not everyone was enthusiastic though. One ex-Dartmouth captain complained that the trains brought "a whole Coney Island of people skiing where you wanted to ski."

The B & M train schedule for 1937 pictured not only a smart skier but one whose radiance was proved by regular runs: "See you on the Snow Train." By 1939 there were "Sun Tan Specials." The snow train became so successful that it inspired the "ski plane," a tri-motor flying out of Boston to Laconia, New Hampshire.

Snow Train Season

To have the most enjoyment you must have proper equipment. We outfit many of the most prominent skiers. We can help you.

CHARLES N. PROCTOR (former Olympic skier)
Manager Ski Department

Canvas Creepers (patented)—$1.50 a pair

Snowshoes, hockey sticks and other winter sports furnishings

ASA C. OSBORN CO.

The snow train crowd was evidently important enough for Osborn's to address them directly in this 1936 advertisement. Osborn chose a jumper to attract the eye of the reader, an indication of the continued importance of jumping well into the 1930s.

THE SNOW TRAIN

ANNOUNCEMENTS
of the
Schedule, destination and other details for each
Sunday outing will be advertised in the

FRIDAY EDITIONS OF THE
BOSTON NEWSPAPERS
and the SKI BULLETIN

PURCHASE OF TICKETS
in advance is not necessary
but
it will greatly aid the Management in providing
everyone with comfortable accommodations if
you will assist by telephoning Capitol 6000, Ex-
tension lines 488, 489, 490, before 12 noon
Saturday, and tell us the number in your party.

Further Information Furnished on Application to
F. T. GRANT
GENERAL PASSENGER AGENT
NORTH STATION BOSTON MASS

THE SNOW TRAIN FOR WINTER SPORTS

This is a typical snow train brochure. Notice that the destination will be announced in the Friday papers. The decision where to go was usually made by Park Carpenter, of the AMC, and Carl Shumway, who had taken to skiing at Dartmouth. They conferred with B & M General Passenger Agent Frederick Grant and Traffic Manager W.O. Wright.

The appeal to the workers in Boston offices was: come north for a healthy sun tan as well as a stem turn. The snow train had an enormous social lure. What tales will she tell on office break on Monday?

Eight

Another Sport Gone Softy: Ski Tows

"Unfortunately the tow (Brookline, New Hampshire) was so near to Boston that it was completely worn out each weekend last year."

—Unidentified skier, 1935–36.

Dozens of rope tows were scattered throughout Vermont, New Hampshire, Maine, and Massachusetts in the 1930s. Most were homemade contraptions like this one at Bradford, Vermont.

These two views show the Woodstock, Vermont tow which operated from 1934 on. It was based on "Foster's Folly" in Shawbridge, Quebec, which had operated the previous season. With an investment of $500, the Woodstock tow was rigged up on Gilbert's Hill. It consisted of "an endless rope which runs over pulley wheels attached to a timber-horse guyed to a tree at the top of the hill. At the foot of the hill the rope goes around the rear wheel of a built over Model 'T', outfitted with tractor wheels. The capacity is between 4 and 5 persons a trip with average speed 5–10 mph up 900 foot in about 1 minute, with an elevation of *c*. 300 ft." (*Rutland Herald*, Jan. 28, 1934.)

Most of the rope tows served gently sloping meadows such as the one at Williamstown. Most tows were also short. The longest in Maine, measuring 2,000 feet, was at Bridgton, but Liberty's was 900 feet, Andover's 800 feet, Casco's 700 feet, Bowdoinham's 500 feet, and Norway's only 100 feet.

Two youngsters from Greenough and Noble school made eighty-four trips on this tow one Sunday in 1936. The tow was 950 feet in length, with a 300-foot vertical drop. They got in a total of about 25,000 feet of downhill running, "comparing favorably with big days at any of the Swiss ski centers."

As most rope tows, the one belonging to the Rockhouse Mountain Farm-Inn in Eaton Center, New Hampshire, was short and served an easy hill rather than a steep mountain.

Hang on! Ropes had no supports, so they dragged in the snow and became very wet and heavy. A rope often turned as it was pulled around the bull wheel, which made hanging on difficult. For some it was as exhausting to go up as it was exciting to come down.

Here, Miss Henrietta Sharp of Woodstock, Vermont, takes off from "the speed tow." Most rope tows had a maximum capacity of about twenty people, some only five. If you allowed only one person on the rope, then floored the accelerator, you could catapult the skier into the air at 45 mph. Later, the Hussey Manufacturing Company of Berwick, Maine, would advertise "the new thrill—speeds up to 100 mph on the level." Insurance, anybody?

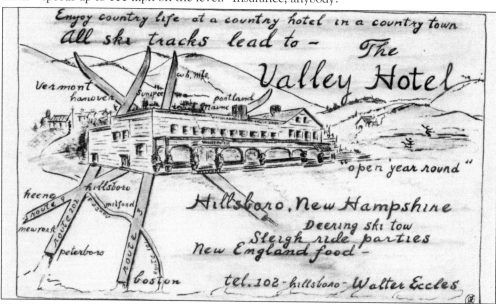

The Valley Hotel in Hillsboro, New Hampshire, emphasized the easy access from New York and Boston, and from Maine and Vermont to its country lifestyle and the nearby Deering ski tow. The ski tow was now becoming a necessary attribute for a good weekend of social skiing.

Cranmore's unique skimobile, built by George Morton and financed by Harvey Dow Gibson in 1938, carried 131 cars and cost 25¢ per ride. The cars were attached to a steel cable pulled by electric motors. The original design used inflatable tires, which went flat overnight. The next season, hard rubber was installed.

When Hannes Schneider saw that the skimobile only went half way up Mt. Cranmore, he told Gibson that skiers had to go to the top of the mountain! The skimobile's upper section was built in 1939 and added 2,000 feet of length. The price for a bottom-to-top trip was 50¢. The skimobile operated until 1989. One of the original cars is now on exhibit at the New England Ski Museum in Franconia, New Hampshire.

The second chairlift in the US (the first one had opened in Sun Valley, Idaho, in December 1936) was ready in January 1938. The "tramway of the sit-down variety," the "chair tow"—or, as the postcard has it, the "chair tramway"—was an instant success and made the Belknap Recreation Area a ski center. The era of J- and T-bars, and indeed of chairlifts, is really a post-1945 phenomenon. The beginning of this up-ski revolution, however, occurred just before the war.

The idea of a tramway at Cannon Mountain in Franconia Notch, New Hampshire, was born when four wealthy Bostonians—Alex Bright, Tom Dabney, Sam Wakeman, and Arnold Lowell—enjoyed using cog-railways and funiculars while skiing in Europe in 1933. They got the ear of New Hampshire Governor John Winant, and the bill to fund the tramway made its way through committees and legislature from 1934 to the tram completion in 1938. The first year 36,589 passengers were carried, most of them in the summer. These rare photographs, some published here, to my knowledge, for the first time, show stages in the construction of the tram; particularly interesting is the handling of the giant cable from rail to road.

This photograph gives some idea of the complexities of building the Cannon Mountain tramway. When it was completed in 1938, the up-hill trip cost 60¢, a ten-ride booklet $5, and a one-week pass $10. The "Sky Route to Ski Fun" took about eight minutes. It was all made possible by a $250,000 bond!

Compare the two-and-one-half minutes of holding on to Ted Cooke's "ski hoist," as he called his rope tow. At the request of the White Mountain Ski Runners (Boston ski club), it ran to the top of Mt. Rowe and helped the Gilford, New Hampshire area as a ski development from 1935 until the chairlift gave it a new boost.

The Cannon Mountain tramway in Franconia State Park, New Hampshire, was christened on June 28, 1938, and, with a capacity of twenty-eight persons, had carried a total of 6,581,338 people by the time it was replaced with a new one with a seventy-person capacity on May 24, 1980. The photograph was taken by Charles Trask, one of New England's leading ski photographers of the 1930s.

Nine

Speed is the Lure: Sportsmen in Action

"I will put speed into everyone's skiing. It is speed that is the lure, not touring."

—Hannes Schneider.

Whirling up the snow, Ted Hunter swoops down the Cannon trail on Cannon Mountain, Franconia, New Hampshire, in fine Arlberg form.

Back in the 1920s, roads were already being rolled to provide easy access to the "thrills" of hill and dale for the "fast" set.

Ten years later, the city crowd had arrived by snow train to populate rope-tow hills like the one at Great Barrington, Massachusetts.

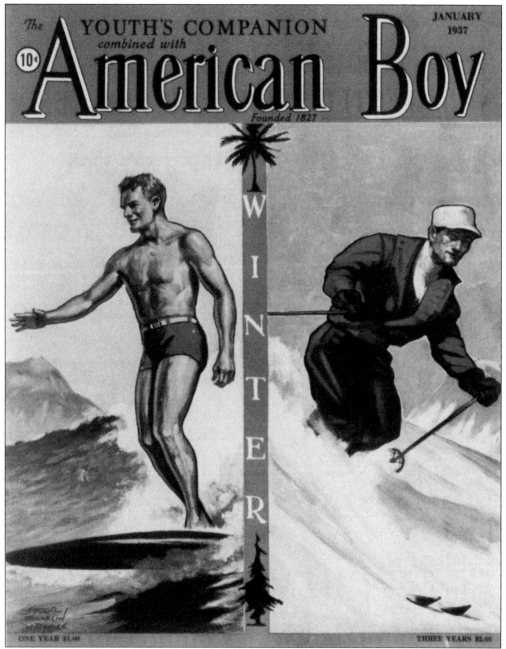

The "American Boy" was presented with a choice for the winter of 1937: surf or snow. Whether you caught a wave or a bump, you got the same heart-thumping burst of speed.

Mt. Mansfield's toll road in Stowe, Vermont, had first been skied in 1913, but after Roland Palmedo "discovered" Stowe and Sepp Ruschp set a European tone, all that was needed for a top-to-bottom dash was snow and a tow: the Stowe chairlift was ready for the 1940–41 season.

Cannon Mountain, with its 2,000-foot vertical drop, had a well-designed layout of trails serving the tram. Banking around the corners at full speed on Upper Cannon, wide, with sweeping turns, was a favorite pastime in the late 1930s, as it still is today.

German trail names gave both ambiance and legitimacy to the New England ski center. Winston Pote, doyen of 1930s photographers, graphically caught Arlberg lean and speed on the Katzensteig trail.

Unlike today's courses, which are precisely marked by gates, races in the 1930s simply started at the top of a trail and finished at the bottom: you found your own fastest way down. To "hold the record on the Taft" Race Course was one of the high points for the daredevils of the 1930s.

The most well-known of New England's Class A racing trails, the Richard Taft, on Cannon Mountain, New Hampshire, was straight for the first half-mile. Built under the auspices of Peckett's Inn, it was completed in 1933 with Civilian Conservation Corps labor.

Here, a smart looking sportsman slaloms tightly around a bush in the 1930s. His ridge top skis would have steel edges to "carve" his Arlberg turns to gain speed.

The woodcut *Speed*, by Englishman Adrian Allinson, graced the cover of the 1934 American Ski Annual and visualized for Easterners just what thrills could be expected from the Arlberg crouch.

The Thunderbolt, on Mt. Greylock, Massachusetts, vied with the Richard Taft as a downhill course, and became something of a place of pilgrimage for the better skiers who relished the test of a Class A racing trail.

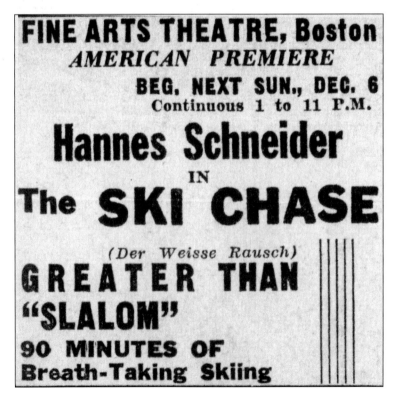

FINE ARTS THEATRE, Boston
AMERICAN PREMIERE
BEG. NEXT SUN., DEC. 6
Continuous 1 to 11 P.M.
Hannes Schneider
IN
The SKI CHASE
(Der Weisse Rausch)
GREATER THAN "SLALOM"
90 MINUTES OF Breath-Taking Skiing

Arnold Fanck's films starring Hannes Schneider (and also Leni Riefenstahl) showed, as the 1936 advertisement for the Ski Chase has it, "90 minutes of breathtaking skiing." These films may have done more to introduce America to the excitement of downhill speed than anything else.

THE
SPORTSMAN

FEBRUARY, 1937
FIFTY CENTS

In this watercolor, Dwight Shepler—America's foremost ski artist of the 1930s—captured a jump-turn off a cornice. Not that there were many cornices in New England, nor could more than a dozen skiers perform like this, but all imagined that they might one day.

As more and more people skied faster and faster, safety became a factor. The first patrols were started locally in 1934. Four years later the National Ski Patrol System was formed by Roland Palmedo and Roger Langley, with Minot Dole as the driving force.

This NSPS poster, painted by Dwight Shepler, sends just the right message. Be of service to your fellow skiers and—of course—have a grand time skiing.

Maine sportsmen and sportswomen chartered a bus for a weekend outing to Pinkham Notch, New Hampshire, in 1941. The more daring would run the Wild Cat trail, while others would head into the Tuckerman Bowl on Mt. Washington. Notice the number of women in the party. Ski trips like this one provided the possibility of what was perceived as healthy freedom in nature's great outdoors. They probably danced the night away.

These women will have more of a suntan than those who went to Florida for their spring break. Skiing was often juxtaposed as a healthy, action-packed alternative to a lazy beach holiday.

From the hot sands of Lawrence's Arabia to the precipitous icy drop of Tuckerman Ravine, Lowell Thomas' adventures were relayed in books, slides, and on radio. Photographer Winston Pote caught him leading a group of spring skiers into the Tuckerman Bowl.

Lowell Thomas (second from left) did much to publicize skiing in America. Here, he is pictured broadcasting from the Green Mountain Inn in Stowe, Vermont, in 1938. Joe Fountain (left) was in charge of publicity for the Connecticut Valley Railroad, and Bob Isham, manager of the lodge, is sitting between Lowell Thomas and Jacques Charmoz, one of the very few French ski instructors in the United States.

Ten

Downhill all the Way: Racing the Trails

"On steep pitches, casting form, technique and control to the winds, he adopted the simple expedient of sitting on the tails of his skis. We are told it is within the rules."

Ski Bulletin, 1933.

Marion McKean from Beverly, Massachusetts, one of a very few expert women skiers in the US in the 1930s, showed good slalom form. She was on the Olympic squad in 1936.

Nansen Club Juniors made the best of bad conditions in the north country. There were only cross-country races until about 1930, when the downhill craze began.

The streets of Berlin, New Hampshire, were rolled rather than plowed in the 1920s. Cross-country races often started and finished in town, where it was easy for crowds to assemble.

In their everyday winter sports clothes and with unsophisticated attitudes, this racing foursome is typical of women's teams in the early 1930s. Here, the University of Vermont women's team of 1933 stands with their coach, Ken Salls: Louise Bull, Hilda Crawford, Pauline Graves, and Karen Atkinson.

The Massachusetts state championships were promoted with a figure whose scarf would be enough to slow anybody down. The emphasis is on joie-de-vivre rather than winning the race.

The first United States downhill championship was held on Dartmouth's own Mt. Moosilauke in March 1933. The race required event "police" who also doubled as cooks! Here, a contestant is taking a corner on Hell's Highway, a 2.8 mile run which was "more dangerous than drilling," according to coach Otto Schniebs, "due to its narrowness with both sides thickly wooded." Schniebs regretted that there was no women's class and suggested there be one for the next championship.

One Moosilauke downhiller came off the top, and then skied a "straight, easy gradual descent. First turn a Christiania. Then steeper, and next an 'S' curve, narrow, banked like a race track, with a solid line of spruce at the top. Instinctively I braked . . . fell inwards, my skis crashed against the lower branches of a tree . . . Up again, and once more gathering speed along the 'Devil's bumps,' hard banks of drifted snow, where the very vitals seemed to be shaken out of me."

The finish gate marked ZIEL indicates the Alpine influence in America. Early racing in Stowe, Vermont, under the tutelage of Austrian Sepp Ruschp took place on the "Nose Dive." With its seven turns at the top, this run was well known among New England racers.

Two views of racing on the Thunderbolt trail on Mt. Greylock, Massachusetts, give some idea of what a Class A racing trail comprised. With the increasing numbers of racers tearing down the hills, the number of accidents mounted. In the years before World War II, giant slalom gates were proposed and experimented with on Mt. Greylock in order to diminish the risks.

Through the gates in stylish clothes, this racer showed stylish form. Early slalom courses were defined by small flags stuck in the snow, then by bamboo poles. Instructions on how to set a slalom course were always part of the ski manuals of the 1930s.

These were the days before electronic timing! Early on, watches were set at the bottom of the course, and the starting times agreed upon depended upon how long it took to climb up to the start.

Here, one of the best known skiers in the east, Alex Bright, shows his "hockey-stop" form. His influence on New England skiing came through his founding of the ski club Hochgebirge of Boston, his membership on the 1936 Olympic team, and not least because the construction of the Cannon Mountain tramway was his idea.

The National Downhill Championship put Stowe, Vermont, on the ski map in 1938.

Pictured here having a great time are four personalities of far-reaching influence on New England skiing: Harvey Dow Gibson, who sprang Hannes Schneider from Nazi house arrest and brought him to Cranmore, New Hampshire; Toni Matt, best known for his famous "schuss" of the Tuckerman Headwall in the 1939 Inferno race; Sel Hannah, Dartmouth captain and member of the 1940 Olympic team, who designed many of New England's ski trails; and Herbie Schneider, who became an influential instructor, wrote an instructional book, and ran Mt. Cranmore after his father had died.

The "gals" on spring race day were all fitted out with bibs and puttees. These are not Class A racers—just look at the way No. 75 is holding her poles!

Fletcher, Cooty, Starr, Constant, Fowler, Beck, and their coach, Sepp Ruschp, made up the Norwich University (Vermont) team just before World War II. Norwich University had cadets in training for ski warfare as early as 1917.

Shown here is Dartmouth's lineup for the 1936–37 race season. From left to right are Harry Cooke, Ti Chamberlin, Ed Meservey, Steve Bradley, Ted Hunter, Warren Chivers, Dave Bradley, Dick Durrance, Howard Chivers, Coach Walter Prager, Manager Fran Fenn, Asst. Mgr. Bob Mussey, and Ed Wells. Six of these students were selected for the 1936 and/or the aborted 1940 Olympic Games.

Eleven

Mt. Washington: Tuckerman Ravine

"We had a nervous time up there, I think."

—Charley Proctor, remembering the occasion when he and John Carleton
climbed up the Headwall and were the first to ski down it—in 1931.

The great bowl at the head of Tuckerman Ravine was first entered on skis in 1914. From 1926
on, there were people skiing in the bowl every spring.

Norman Libby of Bridgton, Maine, first skied on Mt. Washington in 1905. A Doctor Wiskott from Breslau, Germany, had preceded him in 1899. This photograph was taken of Libby at the Summit House, when he and Algernon Chandler had used skis from the Glen House to the Half-Way House and then made their way to the top on "creepers," a type of crampon. During their return, they had skied the 4 miles back to the Glen House. If it was anything like the trial run on the previous day, it had taken some twenty minutes, including "the delays, mostly tumbles."

Fred Harris (left) and a companion made it safely back down to the Half-Way House on Mt. Washington in 1911. He had been leading the Dartmouth Outing Club on this trip. "Started up the mountain about 10 . . . Had to take skiis off in places . . . I slipped once and only a bush saved me from death . . . Made 4-mile slide down mountain in 14 minutes without stopping," Harris recorded in his diary.

The usual way in to the Bowl and Headwall was via the Sherburne trail from the AMC's Pinkham Notch hut, a climb of about three hours. This is a photograph taken by Christine Reid, well known as a journalist, writer, and photographer of skiing in Europe as well as in the United States.

The first major gathering point was Howard Johnson's, a Forest Service cabin. Beyond the Little Headwall lay the Bowl and Headwall proper.

In the bowl of Tuckerman's, you were met by a 900-foot precipitous wall. Lunch Rocks, just off to the right, were the major meeting spot for watching the more daring descend from the heights.

Race Day! The Inferno races, copied from the British at Mürren in Switzerland, have become part of the lore of Mt. Washington. The first Inferno was run in 1934, when Hollis Phillips won in 12 minutes and 30 seconds. The most famous run was Toni Matt's "schuss" of the Headwall—taking it straight!—in 1939 with a time of 6 minutes and 30 seconds.

Electric equipment was used for the first time in the Tuckerman races of 1935. Stringing telephone wire over rough terrain was difficult. Shortwave radio could be efficient as long as there were no obstacles in the direct path of communication. Electric timing connected watches at top and bottom, and could also spring a camera at the finish line.

Skiing in Tuckerman's was a rite of spring. These three are relishing sun, snow, a schuss, and a tumble. The skiing could last into July.

"Ski whiz Sig Buchmayr doing 40 mph on the Headwall" according to an advertisement for Camel's cigarettes. In fact, this Winston Pote photograph was one of a number of shots carefully arranged to illustrate Buchmayr's versatility.

New Hampshire's State Planning and Development Commission got it just right: sun, snow, skis, and socializing with the same right-minded spring comrades in the great Tuckerman Bowl. This is what made skiers a fraternity, "a bit special, not quite like anybody else," as Charley Proctor recalled of his days on skis in the 1920s and 1930s.

Sources

Boston and Maine Railroad Historical Society: 80, 86T.
Chandler, Susan: 16, 20, 122T.
Collections of the Maine Historical Society: 32T, 36.
Dartmouth College Library: 13T, 23, 24, 27B, 34.
Friends of Woodstock Winters: 90T, 93T.
Hartland Historical Society: 12T, 48.
Jorgenson, Frederick, *25 Years a Game Warden* (1937): 19.
Moulton, Rick, *Film Legends of American Skiing* (1982): 26, 51T, 58T, 90B, 112.
New England Ski Museum: 2, 4, 9, 11B, 15, 17, 18, 25, 28, 29, 30B, 32B, 33, 41T, 44, 46T, 49, 50, 51B, 52T, 53B, 54, 55, 56T, 57, 59-61, 62B, 63, 64B, 65–67, 69T, 71, 72T, 74, 75, 76B, 78, 79, 81–85, 86B, 87, 88, 96–99, 100T, 104, 105, 106B, 108–111, 113T, 114, 115T, 118, 119T, 120T, 122B, 125T, 127.
New Hampshire Historical Society: 10.
Pullen, Clarence, *In Fair Aroostock* (1902): 14B.
Stowe Historical Society: 31.
University of Vermont, Courtesy of Special Collections: 22T, 89.
Any image not identified comes from my own collection.

Select Bibliography

Adler, Allen. *New England and Thereabouts—a Ski Tracing*. Barton, Vermont: Author, 1985.
Allen, E. John B. *From Skisport to Skiing: One Hundred Years of an American Sport, 1840–1940*. Amherst: University of Massachusetts Press, 1993, paperback 1995.
———. "Millions of Flakes of Fun in Massachusetts: Boston and the Development of Sking, 1870–1940." Ronald Story (Ed.), *Sports in Massachusetts: Historical Essays*. Westfield: Institute of Massachusetts Studies, 1991, 69–95.
———. " 'Skeeing' in Maine: the Early Years, 1870s–1920s." Maine Historical Society Quarterly 30, 3/4 (1991): 146–165.
———. "The Development of New Hampshire Skiing, 1870s–1940." Historical New Hampshire 53, 1 (Winter 1981): 1–37.
———. "The Making of a Skier: Fred H. Harris, 1904–1911." Vermont History 33, 1 (Winter 1985): 5–16.
Johnsen, Theodore A. Company. *The Winter Sport of Skeeing*. Portland: Theo. A. Johnsen Company, 1905.
Moulton, Richard W. *Legends of American Skiing* (1982), Director.
Parkinson, Glenn. *First Tracks: Stories from Maine's Ski Heritage*. Portland: Maine Skiing, Inc., 1995.